Poetry
in a
PearTree

Ashanui

R. de Wolf

First published 2021 by R. de Wolf
PO Box 438
Gisborne 4040
New Zealand

A catalogue record for this book is available from the National Library of New Zealand.

Softcover ISBN 978-0-473-59891-4

Cover design by R. de Wolf

Book layout by Teira Naahi

Printed in Australia

R. de Wolf
Email: rdewolfngarimu@gmail.com
https://rdewolf.com/
Regdewolf@facebook.com
Rdewolfauthor@instagram.com

Rhythmic Weave Logo credit https://www.vecteezy.com/free-vector/ornament
Ornament Vectors by Vecteezy
Cover image credit https://www.vecteezy.com/free-vector/pear-tree
Pear Tree Vectors by Vecteezy

Rhythmic Weave

Poetry

in a

Pear

Tree

by

R. de Wolf

Dedication

To my Mum, Lydia Dawn Ngarimu, and my dear old Dad, Pine Ngarimu – gone but never forgotten - the gifts of words, learning, love and discipline that you gave us, are priceless. Your sense of humour still resonates within the whanau, kia ora korua.

Foreword

On a visit to Science Fiction author Chris McMaster's house, he showed me a book of poetry he put together as a gift for friends and family. The meeting I went for was great, but I came home fizzing with enthusiasm – I wanted to produce a book of poetry of my own.

My husband, Ieme, has been asking me for ages to collect my bits of poetry written in various notebooks scattered around the house. Writing tutor, editor, writer and poet, Katrina Reedy also encouraged us to create a repository for our work early in a writing course I attended. I am not very good at this particular task – why is that I asked myself? Because I love to have ideas, create and do, so the filing is always at the bottom of my priorities. Somewhere in Australia, Stacey Bout is laughing her backside off, as she often used to sort out my random piles of stuff at work. For someone who can reason through steps to create a logical process map without any difficulty, I consider my loose-leaf filing a skill. To the amazement of the world, my random repository works for me, but anyone else who needs to find anything of mine may need divine intervention!

So, while this isn't all of my poetry, it is a collection of many scribbles. I also explain what motivated me to write a particular piece and share snippets of information learned from incredible local poets I have met. Benita Kape, Teira Naahi, Taranga Kent, Barney Crawford, Trish Lambert, Warwick Stubbs, Wanda Kiel-Thompson, La Waikare, Kelvin Matthew Bayley, Molly Pardoe, Aaron

Compton, Gillian Moon, Philomena McGann, The Gisborne Girls High poets, Rodney Baker, Polly Crawford, Kath Porou, Kirstin Bannerman, Makere Wanoa, Polly Pokai, Kira Broughton, Tira 'Tears on Toast' Ngarangione (she makes us cry with her moving stories), Jodie Reid, Daphne Maxwell - the list goes on and on, and if I include everyone I will run out of page – but hey it's my book!

I didn't write the poems or this book to enter into literary competitions or showcase poetic talent. As a poet and writer, I still have my training wheels on. The collection is a set of memories, imaginings, laughter, tears, hopes and my thoughts or opinions—an R. de Wolf sandwich between book-cover bread. Take a bite, eat the lot all at once or spit it out if you don't like it – I won't be offended. What I love about people, is that we are all unique, with our own weird and wonderful tastes. Art is like food or wine – you simply adore what you love, and no explanation is required.

I have never been much of a follower. As a teen, I did succumb to wearing what all my friends wore to try and fit in (at times). The repetition of music earworms still creeps into my brain, but I love poetic licence, pardon the pun - ignore, break, or reinvent the rules! Good on you, Bruce Fraser, my first English teacher at Trident High School in Whakatane, who taught students to go wherever our creative took us.

Kia ora, Mum and Dad, for the gifts of literacy, reading, vocabulary, and curiosity. I now realise what an advantage you gave us by teaching us in our family home. Also, to my four older siblings, Sam, Whina, Willie and Kerry, for indulging my endless reading, game-playing and questions. Also to de Wolf Whanau, love you all, always.

Contents

Feeding Ika

Lurking in the deep
With your funny juju lips
Too bad I like you battered
Served with a scoop of chips

In a boat or on the shore
You just love to make me wait
While you nibble and you tease
Are you eating all my bait?

I catch a rock, and then some weed
But I can see you swimming by
In my imagination
You are starring in fish pie

Patience stretched to ping
Elusive darting ika
When I land this catch
Hello to my fish tikka

Jumping out the water
Ika laughs in my face
Fish 'n chip shop again
Or home to lonely plate!

Something Fishy Poet

Many of the poems in this book are from prompts. What is a prompt you might ask? A word or words, object, idea, or concept to provide a topic to inspire writing. C'mon creative brain, 'get your blimmin arse moving!' (inspired by Eliza Doolittle's day at the races) I love the idea of fishing, especially on a boat. It offers the fisher a great excuse to do absolutely nothing while pretending to do something (that could be just me). Don't get me wrong - I enjoy eating the fish that other people catch. No scaling or gutting involved – perfect! The poem is a loving tribute to our national obsession with fish 'n chips.

Busy Buzzy Wings – HONEYBEE

Harbinger of life with your pollination
Overworked wings thrum throughout the nation
Never stinting in sharing your floral destination
Ever working hard to feed your population
Yearning for nectar, let's give a standing ovation
Buzzing and building with great expectations
Ecology thriving under your ministrations
Ever watchful, tasked to prevent obliteration

Eco Poet

Yep, I have outed myself as a nature-concerned greenie.
Nothing to do with politics, mind you, and everything to
do with my reverence for the Earth Mother -
Papatūānuku, and the intricate grand design she balances.
I also happen to love honey and find bees fascinating.
Want a definition of work ethic? Look no further than
bees and ants. Also ruled over by Queens – just saying!

Aitutaki

Echoes from the past
Ringaringa beckon
Whangai children
Washed upon grandparents' porch
Unfurling umbilical connection
Soul-sucking tides of past

Vibrance blue
Burstingly bright
Sparkles divinity
Irresistible lens of promise
Helio kissed days
Whispering warmth-laden wind

Fifty years dreaming
Ping the boxed e-tickets
Delicious tremble
Anticipation
Pilot brakes, touchdown, taxi runway
Kia orana giggling

Bubbling, enigmatic people
Crowing chickens
Shifting sands

Ika mata
Strumming guitars
Silken hips snaking

Lagoon of light
Fish flaunting flashy skin
Tourists poaching and pinking
Sapphire sparkle cannot compare
Seductive, succubus of dreams
Indelibly inked on heart – Aitutaki.

Wandering Bard

A poem that pays homage in verse to my obsession with
the Pacific island of Aitutaki. My grandparents raised some
wonderful much-loved cousins who hailed from this
beautiful island. Those holiday brochures with the blue
lagoon photos have enchanted me for as long as I can
remember. I made a Youtube video and lamented that my
ancestors didn't jump waka and stay – it is just so warm
and lovely. Part of my DNA yearns to return to Aitutaki.
A special thank you to the unofficial Poet Laureate of
Gizzy, Benita Kape, for helping me edit this poem.
Sometimes people pop into your life and teach you a lot
without even trying – Nanny Beni, as Benita is
affectionately known, is one of those people. I asked
Benita, who did not know me, to read her poem I saw in
the newspaper at my book launch. Kia ora Benita, you are
fantastic – and if this makes you cry too bad, it's true.

Ira

Birth...

    Breath taken...

        Jubilant life celebrated...

            Exhale, final crescendo rattles...

                Death...

Poetic Student

I love learning. As soon as our writing tutor gives us a style of formed poetry in a class, I need to test-drive it. Just like a teenager pleading for the keys to Dad's shiny new car, I want to take it for a spin. Last year I was introduced to Cinquain, a hot five-line poem with an attractive shape. Although the word is French, Cinquain is closely related to older Japanese cousins Tanka and Haiku.

Lime Divine

In my mojito
So zingy pop green
Tantalising tastebuds, seductively mean

> And to my footbath
> Add salt, lemongrass
> Your juicy squeaking, fragrance so sharp

To muddle with sugar
Zest fuelled play
Minty and swizzled, you make my day

> Complimentary condiment
> Cleanse palate and soul
> Powerful juju when served in a bowl!

Sublime, divine
As you grow on your tree
Dimpled with wisdom and lessons for me.

Muddled Poet

A writer plucked a prompt from a box of objects – you guessed it, a lime! Then that lime was added to a list of word prompts – how zingy. The poet has always been fond of a well-made cocktail. This particular one is the fave of a beloved childhood friend, when made by said poet. She loves my mojitos, and she isn't the only fan. Cocktails bring to mind holidays in balmy climes, or festive celebrations where hair escapes restraint. So cheers zesty reader, may your recital be well minted.

Makawe (Hair)

Makawe – magical mermaids, meandering mesmerising
Makawe – mangy male mane, matted and mated
Makawe – mother's mare, masticating merrily
Makawe – mothballed mink's melancholic memories
Makawe – meticulously manicured molten muse
Makawe – marauding monkeys munching mischief
Makawe – mythical monsters malleable might
Makawe – mirror mimed mystic mantra
Makawe – magnificent! mine maybe messy

Literary Leonine Locks

When my tutor posted a picture of hair as our weekly writing inspiration, mine almost stood on end in anticipation of the lustrous adjectives that would stream from my quill – cue the wind machine. Then I started to think about all the different kinds of hair and went in a completely different direction. I was in the mood for alliteration, which I find fun. Each line is a strand of memory – think Harry Potter's Pensieve experience with Dumbledore and Snape. Where did my obsession with hair begin? I mused. One of our mokopuna (grandchildren) shares my fascination with hair – yes, Finley, I am talking about you. Mermaids were definitely in there, lions, horses, fur coats from The Lion, the Witch and the Wardrobe. The monkey line is a hilarious memory of being grossed out on a trip to the zoo with our parents. Those monkeys groomed each other, picking out parasites and eating them. As if that wasn't enough, one of them wiped half a cabbage on its bottom before eating it! The memory stuck with my siblings and me, and I am still not fond of monkeys as a consequence.

Lydia

Chatham Island lily
Perfect bud
Promise of flower
Inhaled anticipation of life
Forked roads beckon
Sparkling debutante

Baby Bard

There are a couple of old photographs of my mother, Lydia Dawn Ngarimu (nee Grennell), that I adore. One is a black and white portrait of her when she is seventeen years old. The other is a newspaper photo taken of the debutantes at the debutante ball—such a different time and place when and where my Mum grew up.

My mother was born on the Chatham Islands, but my grandfather, William Grennell, died when she was five years old. Nana, Cassie Grennell (nee Pomare), moved back to the mainland, and she later remarried. Bruce Samson became stepfather to Lydia, Joy and Joe Grennell. I visited them in 1974 with my Mum at their home in Woodend, and we went to Tuahiwi Marae to unveil Cassie, Bruce, Joy, and Joy's husband, Tahu Hopkins, headstones a few years ago. The welcome from our South Island whanau is always warm and beautiful. We don't see each other often, but there is familial comfort in their embraces as if our genes are having a korero (chat) in the background.

Whenever I head to the South Island, I feel its rock and earth in my bones. The whenua (land) is part of me, and I am part of it. My ancestors on my mother's side of the family tree have nurtured the soil with their bodies, and Papatūānuku (Earth Mother) has clasped them to her breast in her neverending cycle of life.

Ngai Tahu, Ngati Porou & Te Whanau-a-Apanui are my iwi which means when it comes to Maori words, I will 'macron' and 'not macron' as I please, without rhyme or reason!

Staria 21

Dawn, waka launches
Dip your paddle in the stars
Taste the universe
Navigate your chosen path
Wairua shining with life

Triptych

Uncle
Miss you
Brave heart gone
Laying in Tebaga Gap
Moana

Uncle
Mokopuna smiling
In your truck
Whareponga, aroha, whanau, warmth
Harry

Dad
Clever, farmer
Ngati* Jeru Dog
Whanau orbiting your sun
Pine

Whanau Writer

I am not sure what my cousin and his wife did when raising their children, but they are lovely. Staria is a mokopuna (grandchild) of Api and Malu and the muse of the first poem. I wrote it for her 21st.

Cinquain (pronounced sincane – I stuffed it up the first time I said it) is a simple form of poetry with one, then two, three, four words and ending with one. The trick is to convey your message and imagery in so few words. I am still learning.

Triptych is a salute to my Dad and his two older brothers. Each person links to a place in the verse.

*I was not permitted to say Nati growing up by my Dad – who told me to pronounce my Maori words properly. Recently, my niece told me 'it's Nati, not Ngati' – how the shift in language twists and turns amuses me.

Jeru Dog is an affectionate term for people who attend Hiruharama (Jerusalem) School on the East Coast of New Zealand.

Loss

You are gone
Nothing echoes in the vacuum
Voice, laughter, breath, scream silently in my head
I take the sharp shards of memories from a box
I turn them over and over
The cut and slice is bittersweet
Is it better than being numb?
What if....?

So much stillness in your space
Grief shred me asunder
Merciless, keen blade
Unrelenting hammer blows
How can I be stitched together again?
The whole is fractured
Only time can dull, the razor's edge of remembering
Allow the light to cast rainbows from my broken shards

I will always know you are missing

At first, I flood my well with endless tears
Then, I try to drown myself in sadness
Numb from cold, I adore the light
Climb out, climb out, you cannot live here
Today, I fill my happy-memory bucket
Drop by drop, cup by cup
Your life is cherished here, in my heart.

Pain Poetry

Heart bleed on a page, this piece. I wrote it after losing a much-loved nephew to suicide. I didn't write the poem from my perspective, but a reflection of pain in a mirror. It took me seven years to be able to read this work aloud, but I did so after my brother lost his battle with cancer, to try and release the pain of loss. I only wrote the more hopeful last lines in 2020. During the worst moments of my life, I often write or play music as a form of therapy. While wine and work offer a distracted escape for a short time, they do not provide clarity or release. A box of tissues and a good cry can be therapeutic, but egads I look a fright after crying! Do not believe those beautiful actresses on screen with their shining tear-filled beauty. I channel a round or two in the boxing ring or a dust-up with bees – swollen eyes, snotty nose, splotchy-skinned reality.

Mokopuna

Creation sowing
Puku growing

Life unfurling
Koru turning

Banished grieving
Mama breathing

Whanau waiting
Anticipating

Mokopuna, you can be anything
Change the world, dance or sing

Your earth
Inherited at birth

Make things grow
Surf the flow

No pressure to bear
Just be here

Love and be loved
While stars wheel above

You are life, life is you
Mokopuna, it's the truth

Balm of Bard

I ponder the ever-turning cycle of life in nature often. Each day our garden, and the trees in our neighbourhood offer up visual reminders. The fronds of the ponga tree opening in a koru are particularly poignant. There are many layers to this poem. It is an expression of continuity and hope. After losing my brother, his eldest daughter was expecting her first child, then his eldest son and his wife also announced they were having a third child. The news was like sunshine and rainbows after a deluge of destructive rain for the whanau (family). I wanted to continue Will's legacy of encouraging our tamariki (children) to believe in themselves and chase their dreams, while freeing them from the crushing responsibility they feel to save our planet from the mess made by preceding generations. The pressure and sadness experienced by youth are real, and it is our collective duty to allow them a childhood by stepping up to instigate change.

Nose Knows

I have loathed the smell of pukuhipi
Ever since I can remember
My parents would cook it
October to September

Obnoxious stench
Cloying and bad
Snuck into my nostrils
Made me want to gag

Mum was so sure
I would change my mind
If only I'd try it
And find it was divine

She bribed me so well
Did my dear Mummy
With a chocolate macaroon
Tempting tastebuds and tummy

But when that pukuhipi
Entered my mouth
My body objected
And tried to throw it out

The macaroon lay waiting
She said "Just swallow it, quick"
My eyes watered, I cried
It went down, I felt sick

I stuffed in the biscuit
To take away the taste
Chewed and I swallowed, hasty
What a waste!

I was so distressed
She gave another macaroon
And realised pukuhipi
Wasn't for me that afternoon

When we moved from the farm
I discovered, in English it's tripe
But no matter what language
Still a smell I dislike

I hoped and prayed
When we moved into town
There'd be no pukuhipi
Anywhere to be found

But then one day
I came home from school
My nostrils assaulted
Before I entered the room

I ran to the phone
And rang my best mate
Shoved clothes in my bag
Quickly ran out the gate

I didn't come home
Just stayed with my friend

Hoped the pot would be emptied
Before weekend's end

When I was seven
We went to live with my Nan
Cod liver oil, saltwater,
Sticky porridge, sweet jam

But the infernal stink
Of her rotten corn
Permeated the house
I wished I'd never been born!

My Dad, he loved it
With sugar and cream
"Don't knock it till you try it
Close your eyes, it's a dream!"

I was wary of Dad, he ate onions
But would tell me, "it's an apple"
I'd bite it and squeal
While he hooted and cackled

Still, I closed my eyes
Determined to give it a try
The taste wasn't bad
But nosey didn't buy the lie

The odour of rotting
Is for things that are dead
Lifting lid of campoven
Sniff Nan's rewana bread

Off to visit cousins I went
Outside, fresh air so sweet
My nose grovelled thanks
To my fast-moving feet

But when I got home
I whiffed cabbage boiling
Another putrid smell
To get my stomach roiling

Give me watercress
Over cabbage any day
Even prickly puha
Then at home I might stay

Hitched a ride with a cousin
From the Bay to Jeru
Not long in the car
And thought I wanted to spew

Nasty fragrance wafting
From the boot of the car
Pot of festering terotero
Made me squeamish and blah

Mountain oysters
Sounds so posh and so yum
But when on the turn
Nightmare for nosey and tum

People dived in that pot
Soon as we arrived

I tried to warn them
Sure, someone would die

You might think I'm fussy
But actually, I'm not
I'll give most things a go
If they don't smell of rot

I've tried every cut of offal
Snake, emu, huhu grubs
Green ants, fried locusts
And who knows what in the pub

But me and pukuhipi
Will never be friends
Because my nose knows
Where my tolerance ends!

Reverie of Rhyme

One of my talented classmates, Jodie Reid, wrote a
hilarious story about being forced to eat food (in her case
kina or sea urchins – which by the way I love) by her
Nanny. That story inspired a round of writing about Maori
kai (food), mainly the stuff not everyone eats. I wanted to
write a poem for amusement – let's face it, I grew up
adoring the tongue in cheek verse of Pam Ayers. Woven
into this verse are many of my memories. It's true, my
sense of smell is ridiculously sensitive. I still avoid a pot of
pukuhipi (tripe) by making a quick exit from its vicinity to
this day. My tastebuds have matured. I can now eat olives,

blue cheese, patē, drink red wine (a complete turnaround on this one!), beer and goodness knows what else. But, nosey has not grown up or changed her mind about the food in the poem.

My Happy Place

Conceived, I am cradled
Nurtured in Mum's womb

Birthed, I sleep swaddled
Milk coma, sweet perfume

As a toddler I find comfort
In my parent's soothing arms

At school, I thrive on learning
Fall for the library's charms

Christmas time with whanau
There's no Santa, but I pretend

Music, sport and writing
Hanging out with my friends

Endless nights of dancing
Boundless energy for fun

Nights on barstool or carousing
Hoping to meet someone

I was bitten by the travel bug
So many places I must see

Backpacking with my Eurail Pass
I had never felt so free

Finally, in mid twenties
It was love that clipped my wings

Happiness took up residence
Inside me of all things

Where now is my happy place?
Haven't thought about it for a while

I'm back to loving being warm
Enjoy simple pleasures like a child

I guess all of these phases
Create memories of fate traced

Now to me, a life well-lived
Actually is my happy place.

Reflective Poet

My Happy Place, shared by talent-spanked poet Taranga
Kent, proved a prompt to muse over.

After considering all the physical places I have
experienced happiness, I looked inward. Where does
happiness actually come from? I wish it came in a jar
because we could add it to our shopping list each week.
Sometimes happiness can seem a bit elusive – like that
fish in the first poem.

Often, the wonder we experience on holidays can transform us into carefree creatures. No work or home chores to take care of. The joy of eating out and seeing natural beauty or historical sights. Perhaps having the time to play with the kids or read a good book fills you with a glow of pleasure.

So treasure hunter – a challenge! Take out that piece of paper covered with invisible ink, and explore the twisty-turny route to happiness.

Radio Times

As magic conjures sweet sound through the air
Friends unseen, silken tones, crackled news spoke
Tunes lilt, time beeps, frequent waves, atmosphere

Sonorous voice, masculine compere
Strange man, lone of night, recordings he plays
As magic conjures sweet sound through the air

Invasion, war spoken 'pon our shores fair
Called to arms, uniforms, shattered peace barks
Tunes lilt, time beeps, frequent waves atmosphere

Big bands, propaganda, stave off despair
Girls toil, stockings dance to wireless tuned in
As magic conjures sweet sound through the air

Homework lies sulking, neglected of care
While Dees' top forty enthrals teenage minds
Tunes lilt, time beeps, frequent waves, atmosphere

No TV, nor email, media shared
Family time, poured like wine, comfort of home
As magic conjures sweet sound through the air
Tunes lilt, time beeps, frequent waves, atmosphere.

Studious Scribbler

Villanelle – the word sounds so exotic. I recalled the word from the TV series assassin in Killing Eve. It is related to the much older Ghazal. A villanelle is an intriguing form of poetry with a repeated refrain in a set pattern. As soon as I read about it, I knew I would write one. When I looked for examples of the villanelle, I was familiar with Dylan Thomas' work 'Do not go gentle into that good night', which is one of the most well-known modern examples. It is my first attempt, and no doubt, like most activities, I will get better at it if I practice. I like to push myself out of my comfort zone, and I am pretty proud of myself for giving this a go. Hurrah! I am addicted to Black Adder, and I always hear Rick Mayall, who played Lord Flashheart, leading the cast in 'Hurrah!' when Black Adder is about to marry a boy called Bob – short for Kate. You really should watch that episode for a laugh.

Tahi – 3 Line Protest
Children thrown to ground
No title Rangatira
Mana, values, lived

Rua - World Politics – Rise of the Anti-Rangatira
Who put you in charge?
Bad haircut
Bagged wind
Superior attitude
Self-absorbed
Stuffed shirt
Money lined shoes
Words say nothing
Blah blah blah
Remembered a buffoon

Toru - True Calling
Rangatira
Can you hear
The conch wind
Atua beckon
Mana blessed
New future to be limned
Rangatira
Come forward, take up your cloak
Tīpuna whisper
Sands shift
Earth scorched and smote

Rangatira
It's time
To answer your call
Aroha lit
Enlightened carer
Guiding waka, stand tall
Rangatira
Reconnect us
To whenua of our birth
Mauri
Pulsing hope
Reverence of mother earth
Rangatira
Haere mai
Change the world, touch the sky

Follow the Leader Poet

1. Tahi – I am very bloody unhappy (apologies for the language, Mum) that children placed in government care are beaten, subjected to <u>strip</u> searches and denied fundamental human rights – grrrr. And what happened when the media aired the story in May? The government stated that they would work on stopping it by Christmas! I felt disillusioned that tamariki (children) in this country are denied basic human rights by the institutions established to care for them. The strip-search issue came hard on the heels of the police photographing Maori and Pasifika youth without reason or permission. By the way, what did you do with that information? My husband is

unable to get over this one. Tahi is the three-line embodiment of my anger. I had no idea how angry I was until I wrote this. It is also a challenge to those who call themselves leaders to wear and live leadership with mana. I do not write a lot of protest poetry, but sometimes the political spin and poli-speak diminishes people without them realising it. I acknowledge that politics is a tough job for people who care, but towing the party line at the expense of humanity is <u>never</u> acceptable. For someone who doesn't underline words often, this is an outstanding precedent for me.

2. Rua – I wrote this before Greta's blah blah blah, but it is written about the same people – you know who they are. When political leadership becomes synonymous with self-interest, polls, or eternal power and wealth, you get Anti-Leadership.

3. Toru - A call to youth that the time is coming when you will take the reins. Youth represent hope for the future of the human race - and you have better haircuts than the buffoons. However, it does not excuse anyone over the age of 40 from taking action now and supporting change. If you make a mess in the kitchen cooking, you should clean it up yourself.

Enough grumpy poet! It's exhausting, so better to do something and put your black marks on this white page.

Stone Teeth

Born
Aeons past
Ejected violently forth
Earth twisting, Ruamoko stamps
Volcanic temper roars
Sizzling arc
Down
Water
Icy shock
Cooling cells contract
Punching, plunging, Tangaroa enfolds
Restless waves abrade
Smoothing cares
Pebble
Beach
Clinging sand
Bereft, wave abandoned
Embracing arms wrap, Papatuanuku
Karanga calling gulls
Scurrying crab
Friend
Child
Flotsam jetsam
Gleaming pebble beckons
Collected treasure pocket-stowed
Hand stroking texture
Car bound
Home
Man
Breath spent

Returned to earth
Life's accumulated detritus sorted
Unwanted items discarded
Mokopuna claimed
Stone
River
High tide
Mirror skin reflects
Arm drawn stone skimmed
Skip, skip, plunk
Tears well
Born

Shape-Shifting Scribbler

My writing teacher, Katrina Reedy, lifts our lazy eyelids to see possibilities we weren't contemplating. There was I so immersed in the words that I hadn't thought about the shape of my poetry. Thank you, Trish Lambert, for the marvellous boat 'Sailing to Waiheke', a classic example of calligram and the inspiration for the Stone Teeth of my Taniwha (a mythical Maori creature).

The Dark Side of the Sun

The sun draped golden cloak round my shoulders
Kissed my goose-bumped skin
So kind, to soothe the bite of cool water
Tepid air, for me to bathe in

Shining radiant through closed lids,
I smiled at the gentle caress
No more swimming for me, in that cold stream
Being warm is what I love best

The droning of insects, so busy at work
Water bubbling up from the deep
I drooped and soon slipped into dream
Seduced by that succubus sleep

Time flowed on, racing with water
To rendezvous with the sea
I slumbered on, devoid of care
My dreams rosy-tinted you see

And while I slept, the sun flayed my skin
Strokes of whip-sharp, golden rays
My tan turned red, so raw and so sore
I wouldn't sleep soundly for days

Stumbling home in a haze of pain
Gasps escaped at my door
My Mum was distraught, my Dad looked stricken
And Nanny gave me what for!

Aue! By kare! What have you done?
Get your clothes off and in a cold bath
Your waewae are paru, scrub with the brush
Your cousin needs a kick up the arse!

My skin and my body soon went separate ways
Shedding ribbons in translucent strips
Picking at bubbles and scratching the edges
Distracted from cracked, blistered lips

For the rest of the summer, my sleeves were long
Ankle-skimmed skirts swished the ground
I begged for shorts, singlets and togs

"Not for you, sunstroke girl" Mama frowned

Now in the summer, I cover myself
My parents perpetually stern
Scarred, I wear hat, zinc, and blouse
Beware sun's brutal kiss and its burn

Waewae = legs, paru = dirty, Aue! = Good grief (in this context), By kare! = What the heck! (in this context)

Sun-stroked Scribe

A poem that is and isn't a true story. More a patchwork of
summer occurrences that I have stitched into a poetic

quilt. Let's face it most of us have, unfortunately, experienced the pain of overindulging in our fierce sun. Walks, swimming or making hay that just went on too long for your skin.

There is a tribute to my Nanny Maraea in here. Nanny was fond of throwing us all into her big old-fashioned bathtub and scrubbing us till we were pink. It was a painful experience because she wielded her scrubbing brush with a firm hand. Hands that raised broods of children, birthed and whangai (Maori adopted), and kept them all in line with her whip-crack voice. She was a legend our Nanny, a stern matriarch, and we loved her dearly.

Get your sunscreen on whanau!

Matariki Twins

Where did you come from
Bright blue stars
444 light years
I guess it's not so far

Hanging low
Your burning cluster
Bove Pohutukawa
Lament those passed – we luv ya

Chorus One	Chorus Two
Waitī	Waitā
Shine on me	Shine on me
Who knows	Always moving
Just where your rivers flow	Restless sea
Springs and lakes	Waves and ripples
Verdant valleys	Heaving swelling
Its your creatures	Kaimoana
Who fill our bellies	That fills our bellies

Matariki twins
Welcome New Year
Tell us when to
Gather this year

Small swift gifts
Make our world go round
While you burn on
Distant but so profound

Where did you come from
Bright blue stars
444 light years
I guess it's not so far

*For my pakeha friends and framily (yes, it's intentional – love that word),
Maori words used in the context of this poem.*
*Whakapapa = genealogy, Tīpuna/Tupuna = ancestors, Waka = traditional
canoe, Whenua= land, Aotearoa = NZ, Taonga = treasure, Tamariki = children,
Whanaunga - relative*

Melody Maker

I wrote a song when we were researching Matariki, the
Maori New Year. My topic was the twin stars. The tune is
on YouTube, R de Wolf Author. Chords C-G-Em-Am-D

Universal Whakapapa

Earth of my bones
History-flow veins
Whakapapa stamped genes
Entwined with our names

From Taiwan or elsewhere?
Pacific scattered seed
DNA evolving
Culture and creed

Tīpuna paddle
Waka navigates ashore
Whenua embracing
Mystic Aotearoa

Pohutukawa flourishes
New branches of tree
Weaving stories, the fabric
Of our genealogy

Lines surge and diminish
Skeletons hidden at times
Colonial guilt-trips
Subvert truth from minds

Branches or vines?
Choking earth and nations
Burning and clearing
For exploding populations

Inventive mother
She snips and she prunes
Wrap her in plastic
Tight, til she swoons

Weighty and wieldy
How fast grows that tree
Choices for some
No such luck for many

Children spawned, spurned
Hungry, abused in this world
Forgotten taonga
Potential left unfurled

Mother Earth is crying
Battered and used
Tamariki traumatised
Look to adults confused

Java man, seven tribes
Mitochondrial Eve
Double helix combined
To produce you and me

Stars explode
Elements mingle, protein
Cells divide, multiply
Links to Lucy, our Eve

We are one people
Shared whakapapa you see

Universe descended
All humanity

Footnote:
So whanaunga, dear relos
Shall we clean up our act?
If we screw up the planet
There's no coming back...

Sentinel Scribe

It is a poem that wends its way from our Polynesian origins and discusses questions raised regarding the theory we came from Taiwan when pottery is discovered elsewhere - to an environmental plea for everyone to clean up our planet. The fourth stanza speaks to the flourishing Maori society before colonisation, while the next stanza covers a surging European and diminishing native population as disease spread. Religion arrived and introduced concepts such as incest, discouragement of the marriage of closely related people. Maori often married close to preserve guardianship of the land. Skeletons in the closet refers to the hiding of whakapapa (genealogy) that occurred to cover up relationships that were suddenly deemed shameful by the church. The following verses are about population explosion, pandemics and the rise of plastics. The 'choices' line refers to a couple of issues—the privilege of having choices about your body and birth control. I have Irish blood, and it was undoubtedly a relief for my Irish cousins to finally have the right to own their bodies. I was a UNICEF global parent for many years, and the amount of neglected children in the world is truly heartbreaking. The 'looking to adults confused' line reflects the disappointment and loss of faith our youth have in government and adults to address climate change. They are frustrated with talkfests and inaction. The poem ends with a focus on our commonality rather than the differences we often obsess over.

Wings of Fire

Once vibrant, majestic
Now, cold ashes forlorn
Grey carbon, wind scattered
But you shall be reborn

Life stirs hopeful in hearth
Destiny to unfold
Arise, cry defiance
Squawk, confidence so bold

For your life will be long
Mythic creature, fire-bird
Majestic beak raised song
Message trumpets well heard

Feathers rippled, from flame
Uplift wings, reach for sky
Soar with Zephyr above
Beating magic on high

Take me with you Phoenix
Wind-whoosh tugs my hair
Though mere mortal I am
Heaven inspires no fear

Writing Wings

What a fantastic prompt – wings. My mind was soaring as soon as I spied the letters on the Turanganui Poets Collective page. I forgot that I had written this poem as I also wrote an acrostic poem, HONEYBEE, which I love. Katrina Reedy also posted a poem about her mother, and I was temporarily lost in the beauty of her wings. Then the dulcet tones of Molly Pardoe captivated me with 'Wings From My Kitchen Window'.

Perhaps, I didn't recall my dear Phoenix because the image is laced with fiery pain. Phoenix was the name of my brother Will's band – a name I chose. It recalls teenage days of playing music, singing, dancing, driving to and from gigs with Willy Weka, Alan, Doc & Eileen. But the contrast of that carefree youth, to life without my brother, is honey to a bee sting.

Still, it is better to have soared together than never to have spread wings at all.

Surfing the Flow of Life

Tipuna displacing,
> carving a path through oceans and heavens

Souls ever-reaching for distant shores
> Want, need, desire to discover

Adventurers, explorers, navigators
> Blue, merging to green

The heavens to heart
> Speak to me of your history

Waves whispering secrets past
> Where do you voyage now?

Still, we carve the way mokopuna
> Not time yet for you

To be wrapped in the seaweed of souls
> Surf the curl of existence

Currents pull
> Ebb and flow

Ira

Ekphrastic Poet Enthusiast

At 54, I had no idea what an ekphrastic poem was. I thought the word looked Greek. It does come from the Greek word ekphrasis, which means writing about a piece of art. Our intrepid tutor took us on an excursion to a local gallery, Toi Ake. It was an inspiring visit. The gallery allowed us to sit, write, take photographs and be nourished by their creative space – Nga mihi.

I wrote three pieces that day – phew! This poem is the first one I wrote. The art piece is a painting in greens and blues, accompanied by a feather. If you are ever in Turanganui-a-Kiwa/Gisborne, go to The Ballance Street Village, have a look and see if you can spot it.

I have written a couple of fiction novels. Guardians of the Ancestors is about Marama, a feisty young woman, and encompasses our (Maori) Pacific journey from Hawaiki to Aotearoa/New Zealand. The second novel is The Future Weavers, set in Aotearoa, and I was writing the third book in the series, Brothers in Whalesong, when I visited the gallery. Surfing the Flow of Life, curled out of my books, mingled with the painting, and trickled out my pen as words.

Wharenui

Memories
From the meeting house
Dipping brush
Tracing curve
Patterns repeating
Black of earth – whenua
White of light – mauri
Red of blood – tipuna
House of home
Art of whanau
Enduring

Writing Black Marks on a Blank Page

Poem number two from Toi Ake Gallery. The art piece is a black, white and red painting. It transported me back in time to Whareponga Marae. When we lived with my Nanny at Pohatukura (1974-77), my parents were involved in fundraising and working bees to maintain the wharenui, Materoa. The wharenui bears the name of one of my female ancestors, and I am proud of the strong women in my whakapapa (family tree). Although I was only 8 or 9 years old, I helped my father mix the concrete and make new steps. My cousin Brian, quite an artist, was inside repainting the beams – patterns repeating.

Whenua - land, mauri – spirit, tipuna – ancestor singular, whanau – family. While the poem consists of just a few words, it expresses who I am, where I came from, and the endurance of family and culture.

Papatuanuku O'Clock

Tikanga ticking
Own time
Marching to the cadence of nature's beat
Calendar of the heavens
No Roman footsteps upon our whenua
Absent, Gregorian chants
Southern skies devoid of shifting Easter
Miscalculated timing, unnoticed by Matariki
Stars wheeling
Karanga of seasons
Earth pulsating in rhythm
One true clock

Adventure Art

Work number three from Toi Ake is about a trio of acrylic art pieces. There is a form of poetry made famous by Richard Hugo. When you write about something other than what you see – I call it inspiration on a tangent. I started writing this poem before I had heard of Richard Hugo because when I looked at the acrylic trio, they reminded me of the inside of a watch or clock.

I am poking at the European calendars and the audacity of man to try and control time. It is also a salute to Papatuanuku-Earth Mother and the enduring wild heart-beat of nature. The poet questions why we have adopted a Gregorian calendar under our southern night sky. The

Gregorian calendar replaced the Roman calendar because Pope Gregory wanted to move Easter. They miscalculated the calendar, and we ended up with a leap year to correct it. Nature and the Maori calendar, however, tell us when to plant, based on the position of the stars and how the moon may affect us, to name just a couple of things.

The One True Clock is nature, and the other a manufactured invention to stress people out.

Aroha

Thoughtful care giving
Selfless consideration
 to others gifted
Compassionately mindful
Sharing, exposed naked heart

Loving Lines

Poets will never tire of writing about love. When faced with the many facets of aroha (love), I was overwhelmed. What could I choose to write about that hadn't been done already by poetic giants? I gnawed my lip, and thunk and thunk. Shakespeare and Wordsworth haunted my dreams, while Pam Ayers quipped and sipped on wine in the corner. I pared back my sonnet, epic, quatrain, and iambic pentameter to nibble on the nub of 'what is aroha?' – and I landed on expressed simplicity.

Strawberry Days

Click-clack, anticipation locked in
Drive twenty long minutes from home
Screech into the car park, grab a container -
Wait! You must register you know!

A splash of vermillion joy in the paddock,
hiding neath glossy leaves
Seed-dimpled, succulent orbs abound,
An enticement to nature's thieves

Up wafts summer's heavenly scent,
tantalising the enraptured nose
Saliva flows over greedy tongue
Earth dusts my scurrying toes

Furtively, I glance left to right
Nobody is looking at me
Pregnant with juice, a promise of bliss
Hanging exposed to see

I cradle warmed berry in hot little hand
Snap! In a moment it's plucked
Fingers to lips, opened in maw
Between teeth and tongue it is tucked

Squeezing flesh, gently in mouth
Juice oozes out in a spurt
The taste is divine, better than ice-cream
Perhaps a few more wouldn't hurt?

Container forgotten, I hunt and I stalk
Skipping light-heart row to row
Time elapses, drunkard on berries
Dad calls "Hey, it's time to go."

Empty-vessel, neglected and hollow
I jump up in startled surprise
My mouth is stained with trickled juice
Surely, we just arrived?

Up to the weighing machine we march
Everyone surrenders their berries
Sheepishly, I proffer my nothing
Shrug my shoulders, for I haven't any

Behind the counter she raises her brows
Eyes crinkled in obvious glee
"Strawberries are yum, I can eat them all day,
I hope you left some for me?"

Pink-faced I smile shyly, grateful for kindness
Dad grabs his wallet to pay
He rumples my hair, everyone laughs
A wonderful strawberry day!

Writer of Remember When

In 1978 my family moved from the East Coast to the Bay of Plenty. I started primary school in Ohope, and every weekend was an adventure of exploration with my parents. It was a golden time in our lives, filled with lovely memories of gathering mussels at Ohiwa Harbour, hiking through fern-filled forests, Big Dig adventures at Ohope Beach, massive ice-creams from the Ice-Cream Parlour (now gone, unfortunately), buying huge bags of apples from the orchards along the Te Teko straights and berry picking at Julian's Berry Farm in Whakatane. My obsession with berries was fuelled by the 'Pick Your Own' concept, and my puku (stomach) didn't have a full button when it came to strawberries.

When I returned to poetry, this was one of the first poems I wrote about summer, and I suspect the intrepid Benita Kape will have a fun time with it. A loving tribute to my parents, Pine and Lydia Ngarimu, for the joy and simple pleasures we shared when I was a child.

Footnote: There is always someone who spots some sexual innuendo where none was intended – you know who you are! The poem is as sweet as strawberry juice, with no smut intended.

Korowai

Kiwi feather
Silky whakapapa
Woven threads
Gifted aroha
Enfolding you, Lydia
Great-grandfather's korowai

Remembrance Writer

On an afternoon of musing, my mother told me about looking after her grandfather as a child. She loved him and he spoiled her. He gifted her a small kiwi feather cloak. It isn't in the best condition anymore but it meant a lot to Mum. In turn, she gifted it to my brother - aroha passing from generation to generation.

Reborn

Hold your lips to my soul
Breath stirs eddying currents
I cast off my boat
Launch into the unknown
Where will we go?
Have faith – you don't need to know
Live for the journey
The adventure
Exult in discovery
Exploration
Life is experience
Not a destination

Philosophical Poet

Now and again, I rebel against having a plan, and I just
want to be. At other times, I am a cork tossed on a restless
sea with no direction – totally out of control of life. This
poem makes me feel better about either situation, and I
have shared it with several friends existing in a state of
flux.

Glasses of Perspective (pantoum)

Peer long, through the glass of rose-tinted lens
The positive viewpoint from high sublime
Reflection, laughter, the joy of friends
Truth, honesty, care, stand lasting in time

The positive viewpoint from high sublime
To those with abundance, what they desire
Truth, honesty, care, stand lasting in time
A glass half full, shared, sipped to inspire

To those with abundance, what they desire
Spare thought for have-nots, small deeds mean a lot
A glass half full, shared, sipped to inspire
Life, nature, precious gift, twisted in knot

Spare thought for have-nots, small deeds mean a lot
No glory spent hours pursuing the trends
Life, nature, precious gift, twisted in knot
Peer long, through the glass of rose-tinted lens.

Serendipitous Scribble

I had no idea that pantoum existed. My tutor mentioned it in a long string of different forms of poetry in a writing class. Because I had never heard of it, I googled it as all good nerds do. A form of poetry that originated in Malaysia, I was intrigued. I worked in Kuala Lumpur a lot at one time in my life, and I enjoy the depth and subtlety of Asian art forms. When I researched the original form of the pantoum (a younger word and description of French origin), I knew I wanted to try and write one with a focus on the traditional. For my first attempt, I am pleased with the result. The repetition of the lines should transform in meaning as you move from verse to verse. Pantoum took me to places I didn't expect to go. As a form of poetry, I can only say that you will wander and journey in thought, plumbing your emotions for inspiration. Give it a try at least once, poets.

Birthday Poem for Penny

Penny
Patience personified
Loving, supportive, calm
Birthday filled with Aroha
Mum

Penning for a Penny

Words cannot express how much I admire mothers. I haven't birthed any children, so I can sometimes choose which kids I spend time with. Not so for Mums. It is a 24 hour, seven days a week job that lasts for life, without pay and sometimes as a Sole Trader. Mothers everywhere, please take a bow. Without you, none of us would exist.

I wrote this poem for my nephew's wife, Penny, for her birthday. She delivered two beautiful, high-energy, entertaining girls into the world (now a scrumptious baby boy as well), and we love them to bits. She takes everything in her stride, and we admire her calm Mama style. The inclusion of her poem might make Penny blush, but I hope Mum Lynley and her Nanny will glow with pride.

River of Emotions

River running relentless, rilling reckless, righteous, roaring,
rising and raging
Interminably, inexplicably, implicating irritation, illicit
invitations, imitating intoxication
Voracious, vexatious, veritable vortex, verbose vitality,
vivaciously vents
Ever-shifting emotions, elated, elevated, erotic, exotic,
entertainingly ecstatic, edgily erratic,
Ruminating, radically radiating, rhetorically restless river,
rapaciously, rampaging, remembering...

Work In Progress Writing

An afternoon of fun, fooling around with alliteration. Like
water, I let the words flow wherever they wanted to go,
following the downward path of least resistance. Is it
finished? Well, no, but neither are my emotions. So we
shall meander along together until we find the ocean.
Why put an unfinished poem in a book, you might ask?
Because writing is a process, this book is as much about
inspiration and poetic form as it is about poems. Trish
Lambert is fond of quoting the advice of the legendary
Hone Tuwhare to 'revise, revise, revise.'

Forever River

Meandering flowing
Who knows where you're going
Eternally wending
Your march neverending
Rapids and rocks, smoothed in wake
Advancing, always a path to take
River of life, ever churning
Snaking, twisting, perpetually turning
Remember the fun that has passed by
Laughter, holidays, whanau and kai
Love once shared, forever mine
Your waka still travels the river of time.

Wending Writer

The river poem I decided to finish! It is about the river of time and how the people I have loved and lost continue to navigate the twists and turns with me—the love and good times we have shared live on in my memory. I am comforted by the presence of my tīpuna watching over me, no matter how far – and sometimes it was the other side of the world – I roam.

One Night in Maastricht

Dinner was lovely
Long looks exchanged
If only I dared talk to her
A minute of silence came and went
Belgians spoke loudly with chocolate hopped slur

Off to the blues bar
To share some drinks
Perhaps there is wifi available here
I can check my tinder all night
Washed down obsessions with beer

A stranger accosted
My uncle and aunt
Don't worry your boy is in the toilet
I think he has issues with a girl
So long in there, I don't want to spoil it!

Oh, it's ok
He's been at it a lot
Thanks for updating us though
Why don't you join us for a drink?
He'll come out eventually, you know

The night passes by
In an angst-ridden flap
I love her, but I like this one too
Aunty orders Drambuie drinks
Hope it doesn't make me spew

Lips get loose
Accents on tap
It is all incredible fun
Some psycho threatens to kill me
But uncle rescues my bum!

How I remember
One night in Maastricht
My brother will never forget
Got a new suit, I like very much
And a girlfriend to keep me from the toilet

Literary Laughter

To quote Madness, 'Oh what fun we had'. Maastricht with boys - destination Blues Bar.

Ode to the Admiral

I didn't have too much to drink last night
My bicycle tyre was flat
It tipped me off into a bush
Knocked me out so I slept on my back

My phone ran away from home again
Where it's gone, I really don't know
Perhaps it ran off with my traitorous glasses
Or is hiding somewhere in the snow

I love to dance to loud music
We all like to have a good time
My friends can play anything they want
As long as the music is mine!

I think it's genuinely impossible
To have too many beers
After five, everyone looks great
At ten, you no longer have fears

I don't understand who moved my chair
Or how I ended up on the floor
Thank goodness for mates with muscular arms
And wallets to buy us some more

My head is aching, my throat is dry
Cursed unreliable bike
Sleeping outside has made me sick
I will buy a new one I like

I didn't have too much to drink last night
Just danced and had fun for a bit
While I've lost almost everything that I own
Don't worry, my parents will find it!

Comical Chronicler

A mosaic of youthful shenanigans resulting in a host of lost belongings. Many teens can't wait until they can go out to the pub or for some drinks. The amusing rites of passage we have shared with various family members are memorable. But good relatives just roll with punches, offer some gentle teasing, and steer you toward your bed, the toilet, or shower when required. Mum and Dad pick up the tab and retrieve your stuff for you – who loves you baby!

The Kiss

Space closed between us
A thousand butterflies beat their wings in my breast
Fluttering madly
Heart trapped in jar
Soul yearns to dive into him
Swim through warm body and meld into one
Has the planet ceased its revolutions?
Have my lungs malfunctioned?
No breath escapes paralysed mouth
Drawn to the vortex
North to south
Spark to tinder
Lips unite, ecstatic promised dream
The sun bursts
Kaleidoscope colours behind closed lids
Drowned by surging tide
Emotions sucked into maelstrom between
The butterflies sing
My body thrums
Inhaled essence into my being
Absorb him – osmosis through pores
It ends reluctantly, abruptly, too soon!
Elated, vulnerable, scared
Naked feelings, quivering, exposed
Head throws a bucket of icy doubt
O'er the tumbling finale of heart's gold-medal floor
routine
Elastic snap
Catapults soul
Returned to confused being

What is he thinking? Head demands
Who cares pulses heart
Butterflies aflutter without response.

Reflective Writing

Young love and first experiences are so intense. The Kiss isn't a real experience, but imagination at work, to create what 'that kiss' with 'that person' could be. In your teens, reality doesn't live up to what you have read, watched, or heard about most of the time. Like most skills in life, you get better at relationships as you accumulate experience. I believe when you are young, growing into your skin, learning to drive your hormones and emotions, relationships can be challenging – like learning to drive a car. If you scrape the paint, miss a gear, have an accident, don't despair – we have all been there. Poet has a T-shirt to prove it.

Kerry - Happy Birthday

You didn't want a baby sister
It was a brother you craved
You said she looked like a monkey
And were happy being the babe

       Home to Te Ana baby went, cradled by Mum
       Left Te Puia Springs, where you were both born
       Installed sweetly, in the green-bath house
       Wheeled in pram round the lawn

You were at school
As baby sister grew
Most of the time
She was looked after by you

       The constant tail, you didn't grow
       Always in your wake, wherever you did go
       You would ride your horse even though
       She tagged along, so terribly slow

Borrowed your clothes
Stayed in your flat
Then jumped on a plane
And didn't come back

       Except for the time
       You birthed your sweet girl
       Aunty hung around
       To welcome your pearl

You wanted puppies or foals
Not human kind
So cute on arrival
You soon changed your mind

Your painting and art reflect who you are
A talent to create, with which you were born
You see rainbows and colours
Carve cats, horses and the odd unicorn

A busy Nanny now
Still teaching of animals and plants
You cultivate young minds
So they may reach for stars

Thanks, dear sister
For sharing your brood
They are gems, whanau
And like me, they love you.

With love, R. de Wolf

Whanau Writer

My sister Kerry was having a BIG birthday (I promise I am
not telling everyone how young you are). She makes me
the most beautiful presents because she can paint and
carve bone and rocks. An arty soul, Kerry can take a lump
of wood or a palm frond and fashion it into something
beautiful. It's one of her gifts.

Poet chews her lip and frowns. What can I give my sister that will be special enough for a milestone birthday? I settled on a poem that would hold memory and meaning for us both.

Kerry just missed out on being the first baby born at the Te Puia Springs hospital Mum tells me. Te Ana was our family home when my father managed the family farm, Koura station, on the East Coast. So, it was my first home. Apparently, Kerry was taken by the green colour of the bathtub when they moved in. The steep driveway was a slog after school for my siblings, but we loved it there. My parents eventually moved back there when they retired.

I am five years younger than Kerry, and she used to take me everywhere when I was little. An accomplished horsewoman who has always loved her menagerie of beasts, Kerry often used to take me riding with her. Whether I was on a pony or a draught horse, I would always lag behind, my only true skill being the ability to cling like a paua (abalone) – most of the time. I knew I was a complete pain. Without me, she could gallop through paddocks, jump fences and creeks freely. Instead, she plodded along as my mount ate grass, trotted at will, and generally bossed me about.

Love you, Kerry, for being an awesome sister and fantastic early book reader.

Kalkan Thoughts – Inspiration of Sea, Sun, Moon & Stars

Turkey 2011

Sea
Refreshing slap
Cool of ocean
Greets warm morning face
Enticement to wake
Dreams from brain fog emerge
Embrace, of turquoise arms
Soul enchanted, salt-basted
Waves whisper
"I am the sea"
"I can do anything"
(morning swim)

Sun
The sun creeps on sleepy hills
Steals a kiss from the earth
Pink-blush suffused peaks
March forward in stealth
Light claims the dark
In slumbering bay
At first tentative, tender that kiss
Intensifying
Fierce, radiant heat
Day has come
(Dawn from the rooftop of Peter's house)

Voluble Verse

Southern Turkey captivated me and my Frisian whanau on holiday to Kalkan on the Lycian Coast. The wealth of history – local stories, texts, architecture (also Greek and Roman ruins well preserved), and the depth of culture was astounding. Kalkan remains one of our favourite family holidays ever. Where else could you snorkel over sunken cities, climb peaks to Byzantine castles, drink tea while you buy textiles, photograph colourful glass mosaic lights, admire cats sleeping in painted pottery bowls, drink cocktails in an elegant armchair under the stars, or homemade lemonade with herbs in a cushion lounge by the ocean, and dine on the spiced cuisine of faded empires, while the faithful were called to prayer?

The beauty of the Lycian Way was only surpassed by the hospitable warmth of the people. I scribbled in the morning at daybreak, moonrise, after I swam, and when I baked under the stars. After ten years, I have attempted to transcribe my scribbled observations and emotions onto new pages above and below.

Moon
The world awaits
Your fullness and glory
Push and pull moods of earth's creatures
With sea-ridden tides
Silvery spine spied
Above brooding hills
Growing

Glowing
Pulsating light
Announces you have come
You ascend
First peeping, then looking, now rising
Cloak the sea, mercury heaving
Probing beams shimmer
Caressing worshippers
Like a god of old
On offer, floating balloons of light
Reach for you in diamond-dazzled sprays
To honour the rising of the moon once again
Once seen, never forgotten
Oh silver moon
(Moon festival in Kalkan Bay)

Stars
Sweet stars
So far flung
Drifting time and space
Smiling brightly
For all to see
At home you coldly blaze
Live your life
Recalling dramatic birth
Long-lived
Oft admired
By lesser beings
You cluster, pulse
Shine light in dark places
Shooting stars – to where do you hurry?
Our eyes are closed

Wishes wished
To me, you are magic
Mystical, ethereal
Weaving dreams in starlit eyes

Pot of Comfort

Gather round
News to share
Ups and downs
To compare

Rest your feet
Stay a while
Life or death
Birth of child

Joy of love
Freshly worn
Hopes on high
Promised dawn

Take a cup
Tell me more
Story warmed
Gently poured

Romance bloomed
Altar bound
Heady planning
Family round

Created child
Welcome arms
Wailing long
Shout-killed charms

Tarnished dreams
No Silvo here
House and kids
Too much beer

Patch it up
That's what you do
You are wedded
Tea for two

Warmth of friends
Hands entwined
Support each other
Through tough times

Celebrations
Parties held
Singing, dancing
Families meld

Gossip brewing
Tittle tattle
Let it steep
Teaspoons rattle

Stress events
Failing health
Bills a'piling
Lack of wealth

Loss of loved ones
Tears flowing

Plate of pain
Nods of knowing

Pot sits
Often cosy
Full of comfort
Never nosey

I like tea
It matters not
If it's coffee
Your pot's got

Promptly Poetic

If the Ika poem was a nod to fish 'n chips, this one is a cosy
to our addiction to tea. No matter what happens in life,
making a cup of tea is the thing to do. Embedded in our
recent colonial history, the cuppa is an elixir for pain, the
Fred to our Ginger biscuit, and the real answer to the
universe – it isn't 42.

When the pot prompt popped its corn into our writing
sphere, my classmates giggled. We live on the East Coast,
a potty pot heaven. But oh, the choices! Melting pot, pots
'n pans, chamber pot, flower pot, Harry pothead, potholes
(we have lots of those here), potluck dinners, Pot Black –
how is a poet supposed to choose just one? All roads led
to the kettle that day. A centre of life unfolding, cup by
cup. Ups and downs poured randomly, at times spilling in
saucers. Put the jug on, love, let's have a cuppa.

Choose Shoes Whose Shoes

Whose shoes I wonder do look the best?
Whose shoes are inviting more than the rest?

Whose shoes shining beckon to thrill?
Whose shoes soles do you long to fill?

Whose shoes walk the path less tread?
Whose shoes march with confidence shared?

Whose shoes twinkle like Ginger and Fred?
Whose shoes long to sleep at the end of your bed?

Whose shoes can you imagine walking the aisle?
Whose shoes attach to heartstrings awhile?

Whose shoes pile in a heap by the door?
Whose shoes are absent but still longed for?

Whose shoes do you envy, perfectly worn?
Whose shoes make feet feel tattered and torn?

Whose shoes are bursting with stories to tell?
Whose shoes are hard-worked and loaded with smell?

Whose shoes will retire without munted strife
Whose shoes go to rest happy with their life.

Literary Learner

Trish Lambert from Wairoa wowed me with one of her anaphora poems, 'I Can't Help Wondering..' in a Zoom class one day. I loved her poem so much I asked her if I could have a copy, and when I meet her, I will ask her to sign it. The poem starts with the same refrain at the beginning of each line, and I return to it often. It has a melancholy to it and would be played in A or E minor if it was music.

We had a prompt 'shoes', and I was inspired to have a go at writing in the style Trish introduced. Voila! Whose Shoes was born. The tongue-twirling poem reveals my childhood diet and lifelong obsession with Dr. Seuss' whacky rhymes. 'Out damned cat!' Other people had written shoe poems, and their work took me by the toes to various places. My shoes march along from topic to topic, with the occasional flamenco flourish, tapdance or soft-shoe shuffle. Whether it's workboots, moccasins or Christian Louboutins, for me, it is all about the way the shoes are worn. Whose Shoes inspire, to aspire, to fill?

So - this is Christmas?

Deck the tree with lots of lollies
Shop till you stress, what a folly
Quickly max out your credit card
Catch up with everyone in the bar
Buy enough food to feed a small nation
Join the run on the petrol station
Wrapping presents for under the tree
Ripping and tearing it off with glee
Eat until your waist expands
But who can resist a little more ham!
Don't forget stuffing, fragrant with thyme
Seafood treats with zesty lime
Now so stuffed like beans in a can
Then - more pavlova? Asks your Nan

Dishes done, Christmas meal over
Unbutton your pants and embrace your food coma
TV is rubbish, but nobody cares
Thank #*!* it's only once a year!

Bah Humbug Bard

I love Christmas. Yes, it is terribly commercial, and I'm not particularly religious, but it has a certain tarnished, price-tagged magic nonetheless. Colourful lights, presents, excessive food and drink – what's not to like?

However, it hasn't escaped my notice that occasionally Christmas is billed as a summer stress festival, followed by a financial hangover for many months to come.

Gluttons we are, and we sign up to participate every year with tinsel-infused enthusiasm. The fact is most humans adore ritual and pageantry. So Dan Brown, please pass me another helping of trifle while I figure out your next puzzle.

Loose Lines of Limerick

There once was a girl from Gizzy
Lockdown threw her into a tizzy
To pass the sweet time
She drank too much wine
And had to downgrade to a fizzy

There once was a man from the Coast
There was nothing that he wouldn't roast
When he found some weed
And he roasted the seeds
He found he could only make toast

A girl came from the Waiapu River
But the southerly wind made her shiver
She warmed up with whiskey
Which made her quite frisky
But didn't do much for her liver

There once was a man from Kaitaia
Whose vehicle got a flat tyre
He was so pissed off
With a hiccup and cough
His bad temper set his hair on fire

There was a girl from Whareponga
Who fell in love with Joe Wilfried Tsonga
She packed her jammed bags
With some fancy glad rags
And paddled her waka to Tonga

There once was a girl from Kerikeri
She smelled just like a raspberry
So when she was drunk
Even though she stunk
Her BO could make you quite merry

There once was a poet from Kaiti
Who spoke words so eloquently
His tintinnabulation
Was famed throughout the nation
But he only rhymed when taking a pee

There once was a lady from Spain
Obsessed with swimming in our drain
She stripped off her clothes
Dived holding her nose
And we never did see her again

I hope you spent your valuable time
Indulging in the silliness of rhyme
Seven days of the week
Ends my limerick streak
Inappropriate naughtiness - sublime!

Footnote to Naughty – New Release for Christmas:
Spicy food so tasty and stunning
Certainly does inspire the plumbing
Yum on the way down
But get outta town
Now the toilet roll holder is humming!

By the Jester of Inner Kaiti

Loopy Lockdown Literary Lunacy

On the 18th of August 2021, Aotearoa entered its second level 4 lockdown. To be honest, the poet doesn't really mind lockdowns because she is organised, has someone to be a hermit with, and exercises with unusually regimented frequency for some strange reason. We also ate healthily and didn't drink at all in the first lockdown! Our abs fought back against our flabs, and we emerged as butterflies before we munched our way happily to supporting our local food outlets, inviting said flabs back to the party.

But I digress. During lockdown two, I spent a week as the Jester of Inner Kaiti. I loved limerick as a child (I can still remember There once was a man from Ealing). The sillier and smuttier they were, the funnier I found them. So, I posted some of the poems above in the hope that somebody would enjoy a much-needed laugh for the day.

Thanks

The joy of writing and being an Indie Publisher is that you can include whatever you like in your books. That is important when you have so many people to thank. I always thank my husband because he goes through the pain of book-birth with me. The ranting when stuff goes awry, talking to myself to work out problems, long silences when I am on a roll writing – it is truly a journey of highs and lows.

My whanau is a huge support network as they provide enthusiasm, customers, and unconditional aroha (love) from Aotearoa to de Wolves in Friesland. Although my Dad Pine Ngarimu is no longer here, my brother Will, brother-in-law Gavin Emery, sister-in-law Raewyn Kahu, nephews Hamuera, Reno, mokopuna Whitireia, or Ika Keepa, who was my childhood nerdy Sci-Fi friend, I know they are looking down upon me. I hope they are laughing at my funny poems, and N8V Child Hamuera is busting a few rhymes of his own.

There is also my inspiring writing whanau from Ngati Tai Tech – Polly & Barney Crawford (waiting to buy your book Barney), and super-kaiako Katrina Reedy, my classmates - I thank you all. To be honest, they have brought me back to poetry, which I love in a big way. My Tairawhiti Writers Hub whanau has also provided a wealth of knowledge, ideas, and positivity. We are all going places together – look out for the Kaituhi Rawhiti anthologies that celebrate East Coast writers. The Taiki E! whanau are some of the most creative can dooey people I have ever met. Discovering niece Renay Charteris, Cain Kerehoma, Phil Kupenga, Seda Naden, Debs Hancock, Mariska Galen, Steph Barnett, Alice Kibble, Robbie, Renee, Josh, and the NextGen team has been a revelation for Ieme and me. You have to love people who can change the world with love, skill and smarts. HB Williams Library team Beka Melville, Zandria Taare, Diego and staff you are awesome.

Friendship is underrated. I have a bunch of friends and former teacher Cara Gilkison from primary school at Manutahi in Ruatoria, Ohope primary school (BF Paula Heney features in several poems), Intermediate, and Trident High School in Whakatane. There has also been a lot of encouragement from people I worked with in Australia, the UK, New Zealand and Asia. Our friends and neighbours in Turanganui-a-Kiwa (yes, you Gillian and Hamish, Gaye and Robert) have shown up at events, bought books, spoken poetry and just been good sorts. Our Aussie friends and neighbours have been there all the way even though they can't visit yet – Deb, Stacey, Lib Williams of Mythical Creatures Collective fame (advice for social media ignorants like me), Deena, Elena, Liz, Julian, Ella in Denmark,the McMillans, Browns and yes, if I get famous, you can all come and hang out on my yacht!

The last thanks go to our Kiwi bookstores and media who have been a massive support, particularly PaperPlus Gisborne and Whakatane, The Ballance Street Bookshop, Muirs Bookshop, Turanga FM - Molly Pardoe, Radio Ngati Porou – Waitangi Kupenga, GizzyLocal – Sarah Cleave, The Gisborne Herald – Matai O'Connor (now at Radio New

Zealand), Jack Marshall, The Whakatane Beacon - Kathy Forsyth.

It takes a team to launch a dream of Rhythmic Weave.

About the Author

R. de Wolf is a Māori author from the East Coast of New Zealand. After many years living in Australia and abroad, she now lives in Tūranganui-a-Kiwa (Gisborne) with her husband. She is best known for her fiction novels The Spirit Voyager series, Guardians of the Ancestors and The Future Weavers. R. de Wolf's novels incorporate themes she is passionate about – equality, empowerment, the balance of nature, the acknowledgement of ancient wisdom, and the importance of women's rights.

Reg grew up in country New Zealand, the youngest of five children, until Dad, Pine Tamahori Amine Ngarimu, gave up farming. Growing up on various farms, when Pine worked for Lands & Survey, provided the Ngarimu children

Sam, Whina, Willie, Kerry and Reg, with a unique and fantastic upbringing. The East Coast was always home to Pine, and the pull of Pohatukura (grandparent's whare), Te Ana (the family home), Hikurangi, Hiruharama and Whareponga marae and beach particularly, remained strong. She has written about her mother, Lydia Dawn Ngarimu, in this book. Lydia's whakapapa explains why Reg always talks about having 'a foot on each island, and a finger on the Chathams.'

She started school in Reporoa before the whanau moved back to the coast and went off to Manutahi School with her cousins. The Bay of Plenty and Ngatiawa station called to Pine, and the family relocated. Off to Ohope School Reg went, followed by Whakatane Intermediate and Trident High School – wonderful learning years for her. After obtaining her UE, the world beckoned, the travel bug bit, and 29 years elapsed. Sydney, the Gold Coast, London, Spain, Greece, and Cairns all became home for a time. Travel became a part of life for work and leisure, with time spent in Kuala Lumpur, Italy, the Netherlands and shorter trips throughout Europe, the US, Asia and the exotic South Pacific.

Poetry is an enjoyable form of expression for R. de Wolf, and she enjoys writing in a diverse range of forms on a multitude of subjects. The inspiration for this book was to collect some of her scribbles and create a collection with something for everyone. It also offers the reader an opportunity to know the writer and delve into how she writes.

If you enoyed this book, please write a review.

Rhythmic Weave Books

Printed in Australia
AUHW020841250322
361393AU00004B/10